T0063317

THE MYTH OF THIS IS THAT WE'RE ALL IN THIS TOGETHER

the myth of this
is that we're all
in this together

POEMS *by* NICK MULGREW

UHLANGA

2015

Published in Cape Town, South Africa by uHlanga in 2015
uhlangapress.co.za

Distributed outside South Africa by African Books Collective
africanbookscollective.com

ISBN: 978-0-620-67694-6

The body text of this book is set at 11.2pt/15pt in Egenolff-Berner (EB) Garamond 12, an open-source version of Garamond by Georg Duffner. EB Garamond is free software under the terms of the SIL Open Fonts License. For more information, see http://georgduffner.at/ebgaramond/

ACKNOWLEDGEMENTS

I would like to thank the editors of the following publications for publishing the first iterations of some of the poems in this collection: *Carapace, aerodrome, aerodrome/JOURNAL, The Sol Plaatje/ European Union Poetry Anthology Vol. IV* (Jacana Media, 2014), the *Kalahari Review, Stanzas,* and *CAPS LOCK.* Some of the other poems were originally posted on a website called *quotidian,* which I maintained in early 2015.

Special thanks to Jennifer Jacobs and Genna Gardini for their critique and support of this collection.

Lastly, I would like to express my gratitude to the Mandela Rhodes Foundation, whose generosity has given me the time, space and confidence to work on this project. Thank you.

—N.M.

CONTENTS

consistency   11

ONE

feature pitch   14
on watching *Notting Hill* for the thirteenth time   16
maybe-gay   18
first readers   19
barrier   20
nostalgia song   21
whitlow, or, life in the time after cricket   22
Austrian scene, 2002   24
bank   26
testament   28

TWO

brunch song   32
in the Company's Garden   33
eyebrows   35
listicle: top five veggie burgers in the City Bowl 36
to the Greek man in the airport   38
Xhosa practice   39
commitment   40
new fear   45
a June missive   47
Mtunzini dawn   49

MANY

ascension   52
anthropocene   54
breaking news   56
democracy story   57
e-newsletter brand interview   58
Boxer Rebellion   59
boardroom statement   60
WhatsApp circular   61
for the dead forester of Devil's Peak   62
trope   64

truism   67

for no one

CONSISTENCY

it's always the same
sun and it's always the same
sky

ONE

here's a poem that I think would sell –
come on, come on, just hear me out.
basically, OK, I write the entire thing
as if it were a conversation we had on
WhatsApp, like, yeah, Emoji and all,
and readers would read it and be like,
wow, that Nick Mulgrew is really something,

really pushing the boundaries of what
might be considered poetry,
what is considered language,
what is considered just writing down words
and formatting it like a poem.
I'm not even sure it would even constitute
a poem – what do you think? people might

consider the idea, I think; maybe it would
resonate with them, maybe it wouldn't.
I'm not sure I'd mind that much either way.
it depends on what you think the point of a poem
is, I guess: whether it's expression or provocation
or minesweeping for echoes in this confluence
of galaxies, or inside the thoughts of another person,

one who sits at their computer at seven-thirty
on a Sunday evening while everyone else is watching
Carte Blanche and nursing small sadnesses.
I'm not sure what the point of a poem is, really,
never mind this one that I'm proposing to you,
but I promise you this poem would work
and no one would find it a stretch at all. ✌

for A

I would quite like to be Hugh Grant in *Notting Hill*
but there are a few reasons why I cannot:
one I am not Hugh Grant;
two I do not live in Notting Hill;
three I do not own a bookstore

(and besides in twenty-fifteen South Africans
don't buy many books);
four although I am lilywhite
and devoid of muscle– actually the reasons
are innumerable really.

but the fascination remains,
a simple want;
not that I want to be desired
by women in nineteen-ninety-nine,
but rather I'd like to be the kind of guy

who stays unfettered by his disabled ex-lover's house
and has one slice of toast for breakfast
(maybe two mugs of sweet tea);
who, thriving on dreams and monologue,
gives foil to a worldly actress;

who may birth awful scriptwriting,
and, giving breath to Portobello
when Portobello is wrapped in itself,
wafts in unbuttoned Oxford shirt
aware giddily of his own unawareness.

that's the nice thing with you guys
the Woolworths cashier says, loading
into my bag spring onions, pre-made
teriyaki, Earl Grey tea, you always find
uses for things other people find useless.
ha, like your cardigan, she continues,
I never would have thought of it, it's not
something I'd ever look at, but you guys
(*it's my girlfriend's, I want to say, I'm on*
my way back from spending the night at

her place, but I don't) you guys always find
something nice in things normal guys will
never find. I buckle my backpack. oh, where
did you get this, she asks, handling it, and I say
it was a gift (*from a beer company I mentioned*
in the paper) and it's from a designer across
the street, his name is Adriaan (*Kuiters, I don't*
know him personally); oh he must like you very much,
she says, to give you such a nice bag. leaving,
I say thank you in as deep a voice I can muster.

things stolen: iMac with un-backed-up work;
gold crucifix and chain, worn since sixteen;
two watches; hand-me-down iPad; iPhone printed
with a photo of my ear so it played a trompe-l'œil
whenever I spoke on it; miniature icon of Our Lady
from a small Provençal village, cast in silver, bras
en repose, engraved with the legend PROTEGEZ NOUS –
which obviously didn't help. that, or
God doesn't speak French.

at this point I'm not sure who has the bigger taste
for Apples: beanied Bree Street baristas or thieves;
cider-lipped publishers or thieves;
people who buy things from thieves or thieves.
perhaps they're all the same person. anyway, I had this
poem that must have been on the monitor
when the front door was crowbarred open.
it helps me to sleep thinking the thieves might have
read it, then, afterward, reflected on it

while wiping the hard drive clean
in a rainstorm in a garage in Maitland.

BARRIER

this morning I saw a man
ratting about in my garbage
and I took umbrage at him
and I felt odd about it
he was probably looking for food
not freegan just starving
but still I didn't want him to
find out certain things about me
not big things like my bank statement
or my SNP newsletters which I get
via e-mail nowadays anyway
things like my name
things like my flat number
which nasal spray I use
things that would be small knowledge
that would make me morally obliged
to learn small things about him too

wouldn't it be great
if someone did a reverse version of that *Animorphs* show
they used to have on the SABC when we were kids
but like with animals who turn into teenagers from the 1990s
a shrimp that turns into a small boy who runs around
mute, flopping around in rock pools
trying to shove water and plankton into his mouth
a horny Alsatian that turns into a girl who tries
to hump everything she sees
it would turn out badly I know
you don't really even have to tell me

WHITLOW, OR, LIFE IN THE TIME AFTER CRICKET

I

a ring finger rung red:

apt
for I am wedded to
distress.

four equal cycles of
moon and willow,
and six-packed cycles,
leather-bound,
increasing:
20, 50, 90 (in theory, sometimes less);
19, 23, 27 (increasing by four but never a factor);
18, 12, 6 (sans wides and no balls).

it doesn't hurt as such,
but if you pull back the skin
you can still see the yellow.

II

I am nine
in a sports bar where there's now a Hooters
and in those cycles
at some point, late at night,

my beer-breathed dad shouts at a screen
and I start;
I ask questions
and he says:
"a tie wasn't enough."

a tie is seldom enough
is the lesson

and we walk home under the moon
in the uMhlanga breeze
that seafoam air
along Marine Drive into Forest
hand in hand
and at home, Kyalanga,
we slept.

III

when I was older
my father's ring finger swole
arthritic
and in a jewellers had a gold band
sawed from a crooked knuckle.

and he rubbed the scarring
and the impression:

it was gone, of course,
but you could still feel it.

AUSTRIAN SCENE, 2002

under mascarpone clouds
in sunflower fields near Linz
gun-crazed Van der Merwe
unsheathes a knife
smuggled in from Uitenhage.

with slashes he de-roots
two armloads of yellow
and hauls them to the Renault,
placing them next to lager bottles
and passports and the travel bags.

in the hired flat there is no vase
and so the flowers wilt on
the coffee table next to a
Game Boy, three undrunk mugs
of tea, and plates of biltong

cut from a leg dripping from a hook
above the broken toaster. later,
when the farmers call to complain,
through the crackle of a 5210,
we laugh: no one here speaks German.

HANGOVER

slouched over the toilet bowl
I heard a starling through the pane
dear god how slight I felt
under your opal voice
your belltower song
soft from all those miles

BANK

I

you are kept awake
by the foghorns
from Sea Point,
from Woodstock, from Milnerton

their incessant moan,
the baritone low, waving,
intermittent.

immemorially, we
ride from the Gardens;
see the cars passing in

their coils immemorial.
through morning white we watch
bench-pressed Francophone men
slide past video stores, hair salons; between

hand-paint all-day nightclubs; inputs/
outputs immutable. up Hospital Bend, breaking
the cliff crystalline, the
shards triangulating between

the new waterfalls, and
the cars and the cars and
the sun, and the sun,

dew-dropping seeping slight;
slumbering presidential wood
disappearing again at Ladies Mile.
in a half hour by the false seaboard

you point: this would be where the sea
would be, you say. but the sea
never leaves. the sea is there,

immemorial, behind the bank:
between the hulking rock;
under those islands floating.

II

on the ship there is a man
with a wristwatch, his generator
shot, listening for the pulse and
the echo, to guide himself through

this shelf, this satellite gulf.

TESTAMENT

if I die you can sell my books
if you don't have the space on your shelf.
but if you can you really should keep a few
to sell later. some grow in value
like fine blends. got a few first edition
Coetzees, signed Vladislavićes, a copy
of *Welcome to our Hillbrow* signed the month
before Phaswane died. the rest
are probably valueless to anyone but me
and you, if you'd want a kind of memorial,
a bundle of possessions, a record of the
things that entered my brain and fermented;
a recipe to give to a child who
in a few years might be someone like me
but in many ways better.

TWO

BRUNCH SONG

you know what scares me hey
once they're done with the Zimboes
I'll be next
lots of these okes are like
on the same permanent residence as me
I mean what's stopping these okes
from thinking, ja, now for the whities hey
but in Durbs hey it's in Durbs
here's your flat white eggs on the way
thanks hey the Zulus you know what they're like
ja so warlike hey they still just do
whatever the King says for them to do
but you know the Western Cape
the Western Cape will sort it out hi yes
ja just some Candarel if you have it
it's a bit bitter for my tastes

IN THE COMPANY'S GARDEN

maybe it was five years ago,
maybe four
but most probably five,
and it was a day in that year
around the day in this year

when we were sat in the Garden at
3 a.m.
waiting for my housemate
to bring us a bottle of something to pass
round a bench in the drizzle

on the Queen Victoria side among the old statues,
the fountains
and alien invasives; the oak trees
exhaling oxygen; the addicts and in-betweens
sleeping under museum lights.

you had just left me for a woman,
which was new
for me because I was not yet a man,
and we were trying to find something to
talk about that wasn't you leaving me.

my housemate came back after a bit: he'd dropped
the whiskey,
some expired Tullamore Dew,
in the car park of St. Martini's. so we left,
more sober than we'd have liked.

and I remember laughing at him
when two men,
two wide-eyed tikheads, accosted us.
I remember the one leaned into you, alsatian
growling, baring piano teeth,

and instinctively I pulled as he
tugged at you,
at your body and your arms,
as if to carry you into the bush, while his friend,
fat, bald and singleted, circled.

I'd never been mugged before, I thought clearly,
not here nor
anywhere else, and yet I remember little,
just my housemate shouting and me, disembodied,
just floating somewhere, as they snatched

your bag. as you leapt I rematerialised
over you
and still you shook within my grasp; crying mostly,
I think, because it was your makeup that was taken,
not whatever else was around you.

EYEBROWS

I miss you

plucking

my eyebrows
and that warm sting

above

my nose
as you look
and kiss

in all those places that

no one really looks at

in all those places that
no one really cares for

those places that
I suppose were meant for

being noticed

when we think
there's nothing left

to find

LISTICLE: TOP FIVE VEGGIE BURGERS IN THE CITY BOWL

I: KNEAD BAKERY, KLOOF STREET
it's the basting that sets this one apart
beetroot-based patty grilled with
barbecue marinade giving the burger
some crisp beneath the yielding bun
way better than Hudson's across the street

II: SPUR, STRAND STREET
we know what you're thinking who
would go to Spur for a soy burger
but on two-for-one Mondays it's only
thirty bucks for a Fry's-esque carb bomb
with spaghetti onion ring tangles and blanched chips

III: WOODLANDS EATERY, DEER PARK
did you know globalised factory farming is one of
the main causes of climate change perhaps
it's time to think about whether it's right
to participate in an immoral system sometimes
the patty is dry but the setting is world-class

IV: THE ODYSSEY, BREE STREET
this is why Telemachus really returned to Ithaca
perfectly grilled mushroom and bashed butternut
make this a sweet-and-savoury delight between
what must be the best sesame glazed dense
burger bun under Edison bulbs this side of Salt River

V: ROYALE EATERY, LONG STREET
get the tofu and satay burger with sweet potato fries
when I took first year philosophy I wrote an essay
trying to reduce veganism to absurdity to annoy
my tutor *how do you know plants can't*
have feelings still I regret this years later

TO THE GREEK MAN IN THE AIRPORT

I

Jesus I love you on first sight
yellow and blue checked shirt
you must be 80 and spent 79
of those years in direct sunlight
when you're dead they'll use your
skin for high-end leather bags yet
here you are at the airport Dolcé
with a Windhoek Light and a full
bag of salt and vinegar Lay's on your
lap you're just going to town on that
bag of chips just letting them fall on
the floor and then eating them off the
floor and really seriously it's refreshing
to see someone before a long-haul flight
not give a fuck

II

your hearing aid has been chiming for
ten minutes Jesus Christ Greek man
please turn it off

Xhosa practice

how do you even say khosa,
ko-sah, koe-sah, eks-hoe-sa
the x-click is easy, man – just
pretend you have a piece of
chicken stuck in your teeth.
x, x, yeah, yeah, good enough. I

haven't eaten chicken in four
years but anyway whatever.
ja but then you have to practice
your vowels, OK, like xa-xe-xi-xo-xu
I can't do that ha-ha *what about*
this iqaqa, laziqikaqika kwaze

kwaqhawaka uqhoqhoqho
wow that's a mouthful *I know*
it's a tongue twister hey about
a skunk and its voice box
hey wow you're good at this *yeah*
it's cool but I can barely speak it.

COMMITMENT

you were committed today
what an obnoxious thing to say so plainly
as if I have the right to talk about it

earlier I thought about this letter you
wrote me when you stayed at my house
– well, "stayed" is not quite the word:

you slept on my couch for a while.
you were homeless – I guess that's the word
for when someone has nowhere to go. (as in,

*hi this is my homeless friend, my friend of
seven hard years.*) you wrote to me afterward
that you'd left your DNA all over my house

so now I could scoop it up and make
another you, as you put it, "another
mentally-unstable boisterous

black woman." is it rude to say that I don't want
that? one of you is enough. I know I could
backtrack and say, "oh no wait I don't

mean it like *that*, I mean it like,
oh no there could only possibly ever be
one of you" and I suppose that would be true.

but perhaps it is only half-true. I mean,
I don't *not* want you in my life
obviously, but you sufficiently fill the you-shaped

vacancy in my life: more would be an excess.
anyway, my point being: I try to imagine what it
feels like to be you sometimes, but I can't. I can't

know what it is to be you, let alone being locked
up next to a peacocked garden near the capital
of one of the five countries in which

you've lived and in which you've never really
felt at home, in which you harboured a kind
of internalized xenophobia. maybe that's

a current metaphor, isn't it, with the Sowetans
burning down all the Somali and Malawian
shops now. it isn't far away from you, hey;

it's only a couple kilometres from Sandton.
granted I really feel bad about all this. even though
It wasn't my fault, I feel like I could

have helped more, even though I couldn't
have. I mean – real talk – it could have
only been helped by those men not

abusing you, and by those men I mean
your family – those men in your family.
Jesus that is so far away from me.

is it OK to espouse violence in a poem?
would that be OK? would it comfort you
to say that I would hurt them for you?

they should hope they should never meet me,
nor invite me to dinner on whichever Jesuit
sub-Saharan plantation they live/work on now for then

I would take a plough and then plough out their hearts
the way they did it to you. I know revenge isn't fashionable
or holy, I know, but I never pretended to be either.

Jesus, it's something I can't even imagine.
I would call it trafficking if it weren't
your family and/or it were abuse for money.

that's where nomenclature fails, I think.
sometimes I think that I could be
a good man for you, a not-Not-All-Men-man,

just someone to trust, who wouldn't try
to earn your affection with books or
even try to earn your affection at all

or anything like that but give you those
things instead, those small things that
I think people sum up as "friendship":

a soft and strange peace to which you
could return sometimes but not rely on.
I think that might be useful to you,

not just someone saying things like "I love
you" and "I believe in you". I mean, those are useful
but often they're pretty opaque, as you know.

anyway I know you'll get better I know you'll
confront these things and I hope I see you
again but I understand if you'd rather not pop round.

if you'd rather stay behind those rusted burglar
bars for a while I suppose that's OK with me.
as long as you feel safe that's fine with me.

anyway, I saw this thing today that I should tell you about:
there were these men with a JCB peeling asphalt
off University Road like a giant scab, like something

I guess now you're doing with yourself. this
is a strained metaphor, I know, but isn't that
how life usually works; how the things we

experience, the things that define us most are
rarely poetic, rarely renderable in verse.
there is no metaphor to encapsulate an

emotion that goes, oh, my friend is
locked up – that isn't just a thing you can
condense into another thing nonchalantly.

there isn't anything beautiful I can say:
nothing tragic or shattered that illuminates
things more, in the way a moment of morning light

can reveal the crossbeams of a spider's web,
elicuidating itself and the dew. in fact, that
would be a good metaphor for something else –

but not this,
definitely not this.

mother believes
in sino-nasal cancer:
fraternal septum void,
resonant hall of bone.
line those polyps again:
give me a zipper spine of scar;
wash those recurring
terrors of sawteeth and resin.

mother believes
in demons still. catholic
hearts slow in unction,
forked women fear: in gardens
verdant in KwaZulu; in gardens
overgrown with delicious monsters and
earth: red, sanguine and ferrous with
petrichor; where the earth reeks of blood.

mother says this
is knowledge of the devil.
she says it in Glenwood in the church,
in its eternal facebrick and chapel
honeycomb; the stainglass, muggy with
air and alabaster; in which god – you
said – God was not the light:
God was the thing, you said

that was salvation, not deliverance;
no, you said, that wasn't it
at all.

all of this is real, you said.
this air resounds with the chorus of Hell.

A June missive

the day your father died I was in Fulham. I remember
that because it was something that mattered then.
after my brother was married in the Town Hall

that morning I sent you a message. it said I was sorry.
I remember you didn't reply. it's something
I can't blame you for, obviously – it

was a tough time for you. I think it was for me
too. I felt awash in life. I remember walking
drunk down Kensington High Street in

my Confirmation suit. I'd taken the wrong
night bus from Baron's Court. I tried to change
direction at stops that were alight-only.

I sat in a shelter. for a while a fox sat
in front of me, then yelped. it jumped over
a wall before I could take a photo of it.

where was I in this world? this was a question I
knew everyone asked themselves sometimes.
I want to say the lights were bright but they weren't.

I want to say that I remember all of this
in the finest detail but I don't. I want
to tell you I realized something about myself

that day but really I can't. I want to tell you that
you weren't as alone that day as you thought you
were (although I can't be sure of that because I am not

you and that is for the better I guess) and this
is something I would want to tell you, for comfort
retrospective. but I'm afraid it's not true:

                                                    you

were alone as I was.

Mtunzini dawn

for V

the bats hunt at daybreak
with tiny nipping calls,
tiny whistling. at five ring
out the distant ibis calls
somewhere from the clouds.
over the Indian,
the peach and rose of the
new day. the waves,
plump with the Tugela
foaming, overzealous,

umqombothi rich. then,
your snores, full of phlegm
and fermentation, like a
pool pump hose
sucking on air.
in an hour you'll wake,
dear German, and break the
stillness. *okes*, you'll say,
drinking in the shore,
some ghost crabs chowed my gwaais.

MANY

ASCENSION

someone commented on something I left behind
and yet I have to imagine the thought behind it:

a conversation in absentia, some esprit
d'escalier about Beleza eggs and coffee;

like talking to a grave, standing above your
grandfather in the ground, speaking to him

knowing he cannot speak back and knowing he
isn't listening. more like praying to granite

or to the trees, to the old soil in a forest
in Templeton. it's not the same thing exactly,

obviously, because I am not dead,
obviously. not yet. but it's a good simile,

which is the reason for a simile,
obviously, to say something is "like" something.

I suppose this is the point where I quip
something blithe, something soon-to-be

obsolescent yet quotable, preferably about the
word "like" and about how all our interactions

are digitially categorised in twain: things enjoyed
and things not; about how ambivalence is a sweet sin

of omission. but a gravestone is not data; a page
no moor, no memorial. now when I visit

my dead grandfather I know it's not him
I'm visiting but myself, because

I am a simulacrum of him
and he a simulacrum of me

and his name is mine and my name is his,
but he is not anymore,

and I would say I am, but I'm beginning to know
I am not even myself, and I'm beginning to know

we are all similies of ourselves – and that,
I'm afraid, is a much more difficult thing.

"Declaring climate change bad [...] is the opposite of controversial.
Climate change is everyone's fault — in other words, no one's. We can
all feel good about deploring it."

– JONATHAN FRANZEN, "CARBON CAPTURE"

today I tried to think about something
at a university in the suburbs
something big, you know something
significant but I couldn't find the words
or the time or the energy and the
American editor on the other side
of the internet couldn't find the
assurance that what I was thinking
was worth money or time because

that's the thing about writing:
the profit margins are low
lower than selling steaks
or mining titanium
or burning fossils
or skimming off the salaries of public servants
while a million people sit in new darkness
wondering about the denouement of *MasterChef*

(I mean I
didn't get to choose this world and
I mean I
didn't get to choose me)

the myth of this is that
we're all in this together and that
we're all equally at fault but that's
just a lie obviously – some of us are more
at fault than others otherwise it's just
a cop-out for people who do the worst things
to say things like

oh we're all sinners

yeah well
that's pretty obvious, but you
do realise that some sins are
worse than others, right? or

oh we're all complicit

yeah because– well no we're not
all actually I mean

some people don't
drive v8s in cities or comment on News24
or racially abuse people at beer festivals or
picket gay marriages obviously I mean why

does this have to be spelled out for you
when there is too much to spell out already

BREAKING NEWS

the hashtag is already trending worldwide
there is no electricity in Turkey
here is a map showing you where in the world
this is trending wow that sure is a lot
twenty-five thousand tweets about the recent incident
mostly jokes about how the politics are happening so fast
we needed a break says the BBC Turkey correspondent
you know that is all you can do is joke
when the electricity is out ha ha
we have lost contact with
thirty or so provinces

of the country a complete blackout
we're not sure why it's happened
maybe a break with mainland Europe
maybe ISIS here is our other Turkish correspondent
talking in a phone in a taxi
a massive power cut affects everything
but the mobile phones they will all be in Turkey
spending a lot of time on social media today
she says we now move onto Nigeria
the election results are too close to call
we hope to go to Abuja in the next few minutes
for an update be warned this
segment does have flash photography

DEMOCRACY STORY

there was this one day that April
when I lined with you
by the uni theatre
and voted for a man named Terror.

afterward we lay with Penguin paperbacks
and shorn-off pencils. you read Conrad
to my left; her, to my right

purring on my chest. there was old light
stumbling through the blinds, slattering
on hair tawny, copper, blanche.
there were birds outside,
singing their kyries.

Africa's top-rated Instagrammer
speaks to us, unfiltered (great pun)
what do you get from Instagram G
it's like time travel to me, and space
travel, I have a huge international audience
tell me about this quote on your About page
oh man I knew this question was coming

why are you still single I don't know I travel
a lot *how do you manage your brand G*
you know all the things you do –
the photographer storyteller filmmaker
consultant founder of Igers SA most
followed African Instagrammer etc. –
firstly I say no to a lot of things

what's your week like when you split
it into percentages it depends what
I'm working on like 25/15/15/20/15
how do you deal with the pressure G
I mean everything you do needs to
be like amazing aesthetically
ja I mean shit I don't know I just kind of

you're well-grounded for an Instagram
celebrity I like to believe my life is a
culmination of all the right mistakes

Boxer Rebellion

mounted men near Tientsin in 1900:
how did you feel on ponies with legs
half the height of their bodies? you
with your capes, I'm sure it must have
been strange to be fighting a war after
the Boxers killed 30 000 Chinese Christians.
they called this a massacre of course
and the Holy Chinese Martyrs of the
Orthodox Church were painted in an
icon 25 years ago. I mean it's great
that we can learn about these things on
Wikipedia, but really this world is too
vast, this past too deep, for us to
ever really know anything about
each other ever.

BOARDROOM STATEMENT

OK hold on *hold on* guys
so we've convened a meeting
to discuss the xenophobic violence
it's bad hey, a woman was stoned
to death, so what can we do?

OK so we've got a consensus
we're going to be releasing a statement
on the xenophobic violence
telling people who won't read the statement
to stop practicing the xenophobic violence

OK it's a good plan if limited in scope but
really it's their fault they don't read though
I mean what if we can get them to
put it in *Isolezwe* in the sports bit
maybe then they'll read it

OK ja but who do we know
who can speak Zulu well enough
to tell people who won't read the statement
to stop practicing xenophobic violence –
can anyone here speak Zulu that well?

WhatsApp circular

breaking news!! tomorrow is d-day
for all foreign nationals. south africans
are planning a massive attack
like never before!! they will be stopping
taxis and beating up all foreign nationals
found.

help combat it by sending this
message to all your contacts. act NOW
and FAST!!! the lives of our fellow africans
is at stake. a message can save a life.

FOR THE DEAD FORESTER OF DEVIL'S PEAK

oh forester, you found our slopes
barren and windswept and bare,
so you planted saplings of pine,
clustered green and maritime,
that we must now dig up again.

of course you did not find these slopes
and you did not populate them,
and they were not your hands
that dug the earth and slashed
the scrub upon them.

like Rhodes, who yearned for songbirds
of home to sing to his shades,
you hauled convicts up the Peak and
you, forester, you put them to work.
like Rhodes, what you did

was say, not do; for saying
is not doing, nor lifting nor toiling;
for saying is not conjuring,
nor chopping nor burning
the silvertrees in hope of

shaping this earth into the
shape of other earth.
like Rhodes, you died and were
memorialized, oh forester –
but dying is no special thing.

a recasting in case you didn't like the others:
here, an old man – let's just say he's homeless;
he's someone's father, obviously. for a moment
we lock eyes on the street outside my house.
he reminds me of my friend, or my brother,
or, better yet, my "brother" – *yeah that's good*

isn't it – and he's, like, lying on a bench and he's,
like, all ragged and unhappy. and me, the poet,
I walk by and think, *oh yeah that's really tragic
isn't it.* and it is. so I see the main image here:
a man wearing a hat and an old coat, either shivering
or way too hot – I can't tell – maybe scratching

in the tarmac by my Polo like a pigeon, or an ibis –
something avian, anything unhuman. anything so
that the sub-text you read becomes something like,
isn't it horrible, this country, as if someone needs
a poem to tell them that. as if that could escape you,
as if you could escape it. perhaps what's nice is that

this poem supposes a mercy: that you've never seen this
before. maybe that's the point of a poem like this:
to open up the possibility that something like this
isn't happening and won't happen; that this is
something unordinary or just-discovered. otherwise
what's the point? voyeurism is too much art already.

still, something inside says, *look, no matter: this captures what's really happening, man, and as such, you really deserve a reward*. a reward, sure, but for what?
for opening the front door, looking at the street
outside the gate, saying to myself, *yeah that's it,*
that's totally it, then writing it down, then leaving.

TRUISM

      a wave
            can't explain
                  the sea

"Quirky and playful . . . [a] wry satire at the absurdity of contemporary society."

— *CITY PRESS*

Equal parts flippant and plaintive, Nick Mulgrew's first collection of poems, *the myth of this is that we're all in this together*, is a three-part meditation on the ways in which people lose trust in each other, their communities, and themselves. Experimentally laced with monologue, anecdote and truism, these 32 diary-esque poems languish in the small sadnesses of a terminally uncertain society in a socially-mediated age.

NICK MULGREW was born in Durban in 1990 to British parents. Raised in uMhlanga and Auckland, he currently lives in Cape Town, where he works as a writer and as the publisher of uHlanga Press.

UHLANGAPRESS.CO.ZA

Printed in the United States
By Bookmasters